Cambridge English Readers

Level 4

Series editor: Philip Prowse

Love in the Lakes

Penny Hancock

T0134248

CAMBRIDGE
UNIVERSITY PRESS

CAMBRIDGE
UNIVERSITY PRESS

University Printing House, Cambridge CB2 8BS, United Kingdom

One Liberty Plaza, 20th Floor, New York, NY 10006, USA

477 Williamstown Road, Port Melbourne, VIC 3207, Australia

314–321, 3rd Floor, Plot 3, Splendor Forum, Jasola District Centre,
New Delhi – 110025, India

79 Anson Road, #06–04/06, Singapore 079906

Cambridge University Press is part of the University of Cambridge.

It furthers the University's mission by disseminating knowledge in the pursuit of
education, learning and research at the highest international levels of excellence.

www.cambridge.org
Information on this title: www.cambridge.org/9780521714600

© Cambridge University Press 2008

First published 2008
Reprinted 2019

Penny Hancock has asserted her right to be identified as the Author of the Work in
accordance with the Copyright, Design and Patents Act 1988.

Printed in the United Kingdom by Hobbs the Printers Ltd

A catalogue record for this publication is available from the British Library

ISBN 978-0-521-71460-0 Paperback

To Ruby

Contents

Characters

Robert: a vet who lives in the Lake District
Laura: the owner of a food shop and café in London
Joseph: Laura's neighbour
Nick: Laura's boyfriend
Maggie: Robert's receptionist
Barbara: Robert's aunt
Jo: works with Laura in London
A farmer

Places in the story

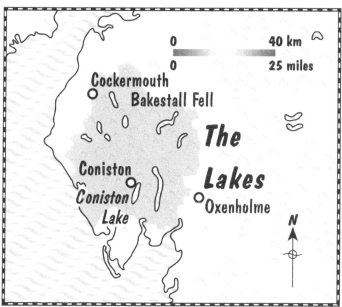

Chapter 1 *The Lakes*

There was a crash. A long, loud scream. Then silence.

Robert heard the crash and the scream as he came out of the woods and drove past the lake. Every day he hoped that he would get past the lake without it happening. But here it was again. The sound of an ambulance. Blue lights going on and off. He began to shake in fear. To his left, out of the corner of his eye, he could see that the water was red with blood.

He stopped the car. He was still shaking. He put his head in his hands. When he looked up across the lake, there was nothing. There never was.

'So why, why can't I drive past this place without the same thing happening again and again?' he wondered angrily.

When he was calm again, he started driving, slowly, towards the pub.

Robert often stopped there on his way home. It was easier than cooking for himself after a long day at work. The pub food was good, local and organic. But the real reason Robert preferred to eat at the pub was that it meant less time in his house, the house that was silent now.

This evening he wanted to go to bed early. He was a vet and he was on call. He hoped to get as much sleep as possible before the telephone rang. There were some nights at this time of year when he didn't get woken up, it was true, but often someone wanted him. Perhaps there was a sick sheep or cow. In the spring the phone never stopped ringing. Sheep were having lambs and he was up all night. Those were the important calls – from working farmers who needed their animals. There were some people who phoned, however, when it wasn't really necessary.

For example, the other day Mrs Fellows had phoned Robert at midnight because her cat, Harry, was sneezing. It wasn't really an emergency, but Mrs Fellows was worried. So Robert got up and went to the surgery.

Robert told Mrs Fellows that Harry only had a cold and was perfectly healthy. But Mrs Fellows talked about the cat until past one o'clock. Robert nodded, but he was thinking, 'This isn't really about your cat. It's about you, Mrs Fellows.'

He didn't say anything. He understood that Mrs Fellows was lonely. It was Mrs Fellows who needed him, not the cat.

Local people thought of Robert as a kind man who always listened. These days he no longer spoke very much, but that didn't matter. They liked his quiet face, and the time he gave them. They called him 'the silent animal doctor'. They wondered about his private life, but nobody asked.

Now, Robert drove away from the lake, and put his foot down as he reached the straight road through the woods. He didn't often meet another car at this time of year. The tourists had mostly gone, and all the locals were at home by now on a September evening. He came out of the woods and tried to think about the good food that was waiting for him. He tried not to think about the lake, or the jet-skiers, or the water slowly turning red as the sun went down.

Chapter 2   *London*

Bang, bang, bang! Bang, bang, bang!

Laura opened her eyes. Blue lights flashed on and off outside her window. She sat up, feeling alarmed. It was still dark. Someone was banging loudly on her door.

She put on her bedside light and looked at the clock. It was two o'clock in the morning. Who was knocking on her door at this time?

She pulled on a dressing gown and slippers and ran to open the front door. An ambulance driver was standing there.

'I'm sorry to wake you at this time of night,' he said.

'What … Who …?' Laura couldn't speak. Her heart was beating fast.

'Your neighbour, Joseph Donaldson – we're taking him to hospital. We think he's had a heart attack,' the ambulance driver said.

'Oh no! Can I do anything to help?' asked Laura.

Joseph was the old man next door. Laura liked him very much and she often helped him. But he was old. He'd had a bad heart for a long time. She had to admit that she was thankful it was Joseph, and not one of her own family or friends who was ill.

'Well, yes,' said the ambulance driver, 'that's what I'm here to ask. It's about his dog. Joseph says you offered to care for the dog if anything ever happened to him. He wants you to take the dog while he goes into hospital.'

'Oh, OK. I'll come,' said Laura.

A few minutes later Laura was standing in Joseph's sitting room, holding a small dog in her arms. She watched the ambulance people carry Joseph out.

The old man looked up at Laura.

'You will take care of him, won't you?' he said. Laura took Joseph's hand.

'Don't you worry,' she said. 'I'll look after him, I promise.'

'Because I don't want Kip to die before me,' said the old man.

'Oh no, I'm sure he won't,' said Laura kindly, then suddenly wondered if that was the right thing to say.

'I mean …' she went on. 'Look, neither of you are going to die. You're going to be fine, and I'll keep Kip until you come home.'

'Thank you, my dear. You're a good girl,' said Joseph, and he was gone.

The ambulance drove away and Laura watched it go with the little dog in her arms.

Then she remembered. 'I'm going away to the Lake District this afternoon with Nick! What's he going to say about this dog?' she thought.

She remembered what Nick had said to her. 'I usually go alone. I like to get back to the earth, do a bit of water sports and so on. But I don't want to spend four days away from you. If, that is, you'd like to come?'

And Laura had said, 'Yes! Yes, of course I'd like to come!'

Four days in the Lakes! And with Nick!

She'd only met him a few weeks ago. He'd come into her shop and café for a cappuccino one day. Then he'd come in the next day and the day after that, and Laura had begun to wonder who this smart, funny man was.

She and her assistant in the shop, Jo, often played guessing games about their customers. They guessed their names, their jobs, what they were like. It was a good way of passing the time when the shop was quiet and it made them laugh.

'What do you think he does?' Laura asked Jo one day.

Nick had just left the shop. He was wearing a leather jacket and a smart, Paul Smith shirt.

'I think he's a bank manager,' said Jo.

'Oh no!' said Laura. 'He's more arty than that.'

'A fashion designer?' suggested Jo.

'No, I think he's probably a people person – a teacher maybe?' said Laura.

'Too smart! A doctor?' said Jo.

'No, too relaxed-looking. Perhaps he's a film director?' said Laura.

'Yes, a film director called Francesco!' Jo laughed.

'Miles,' said Laura.

'OK, Miles,' agreed Jo. 'He directs thrillers and in his free time he goes rock climbing. And he likes you, Laura.'

'Hmm,' Laura said. 'I quite like the idea of a rock-climbing film director!' Jo and Laura both laughed.

At last Nick asked Laura out. He worked near Laura's café he said, as a designer. He lived in a smart new flat. He rode a motorbike and he owned a sports car. He liked going motor racing, he told Laura.

'Not rock climbing?' Laura asked him, her eyes shining.

'No, I don't like heights,' answered Nick. 'Why do you ask?'

'It doesn't matter,' she said. 'I was just wondering.'

They started to see each other regularly. Laura enjoyed being with him. They went to good restaurants and pubs beside the river Thames, and he told her stories that made her laugh.

And now he'd asked her to go away with him, to the Lake District. One of her favourite places in England. One of the best places for walking in England. So he wasn't just a city type, he liked the countryside too! And that mattered to Laura. It mattered a lot.

As she got back into bed, with Kip lying on the end of it, Laura felt confused.

'If Nick doesn't want the dog to go, perhaps I'll have to stay here,' she thought. 'I promised Joseph I'd look after Kip and I can't let him down.'

She thought of four days alone in her flat with a dog. She thought of being with Nick in the Lakes. She knew which she would prefer. She loved the countryside. And maybe … maybe she was beginning to love Nick. She wasn't sure. It was a long time since she had liked, really liked, anyone.

'OK.' She smiled to herself. 'He is not a film director after all. But he is clever and funny and I do enjoy being with him … and I do want to go away with him. So what's he going to say about the dog?'

Chapter 3 *The dog comes too*

'A dog?' he asked.

'Yes, a dog!'

'That dog?'

'Yes, this dog.'

It was four o'clock on Thursday afternoon. Nick had arrived at Laura's flat in his sports car. They'd both agreed to take Friday off work.

Laura stood in the open door. In her arms was a small dog. It had long ears and long hair. It was the colour of that nice paint Nick had just redone his flat with. The paint was called 'Bone'.

'We're not taking a dog to the Lake District!' said Nick.

'I'm sorry,' said Laura. 'Joseph went into hospital last night. He had a heart attack. So I've got to look after the dog. I'm afraid if he can't come with us, I can't come at all.'

'Joseph? Who's Joseph?' asked Nick.

'You know, he's the old man I told you about. He's my neighbour – my friend,' explained Laura.

'Oh, him!' Nick remembered now. Laura often talked about an old man who she sometimes visited. Nick hadn't listened very carefully. After all, the man was seventy-six. Nick wasn't very interested in seventy-six-year-old men.

'Hasn't he got anyone else he can ask?' suggested Nick.

'No, Nick,' said Laura. 'You remember, I told you his wife died last year. There's nobody else to look after the dog.'

'Hasn't he got children … grandchildren?' Nick went on.

'No, he's only got me,' said Laura.

Nick made a 'tut' sound with his tongue. He'd been looking forward to a weekend away jet-skiing on the lakes. Then he'd decided to ask Laura along. He never usually invited his girlfriends away with him.

And now she was bringing a dog! Normally he would be very annoyed. But as he looked at Laura, with her wild blonde hair and her pink cheeks, holding the little dog in her arms, he couldn't help thinking how attractive she looked.

'You,' said Nick, walking round behind Laura now and kissing her hair, 'are too kind. That's your problem. So we're taking a dog on holiday with us ... Well, it'll be ... interesting, I suppose.'

Laura smiled at him. 'You mean Kip *can* come too?'

'Only because if he doesn't, you won't. And I want you with me,' said Nick.

'Oh, that's wonderful! I was so looking forward to this weekend!' said Laura.

'Good. Well, let's get going,' said Nick. 'Are your bags packed?'

'All ready,' said Laura pointing to two bags beside the front door.

'Now, where are we going to put the dog?' asked Nick.

'He can sit with me,' suggested Laura.

'Is that allowed? He'll have to go in the back, on top of the luggage,' said Nick.

*   *   *

'I think we need to stop,' said Laura.

It was four hours later. Nick and Laura had left London and were driving north.

13

'What?' asked Nick.

'Nick, we must stop! Kip needs to get out,' said Laura.

Kip was sitting on top of their luggage. The small sports car was full. There were Laura's two bags, Nick's expensive leather suitcase and his wetsuits.

The dog was barking now. Nick looked annoyed.

'Nick, I'm thinking of your luggage,' said Laura.

'OK, OK,' said Nick. He parked the car at the side of the road, but it was clear he wasn't happy about stopping for a dog.

'It's going to be midnight by the time we get there,' he said.

'I'm sorry,' said Laura when she came back to the car with Kip.

If this dog stopped her getting to know Nick better, she would be so unhappy. But what could she do? She had to help poor old Joseph.

She gave Nick a quick look as they set off again. Was he angry with her? He looked back at her and smiled. He took hold of her hand and held it. And she relaxed.

'Everything's going to be all right,' she thought. 'Perhaps Nick will even learn to love this little dog.'

* * *

An hour and a half later Nick slowed down outside a pub.

'Why are we stopping?' asked Laura.

'We need to eat. We're nearly there now and I'm really hungry!'

'But I've got food in my bag. I brought some things from my shop. I can cook when we arrive.'

Laura felt disappointed. Cooking was her great love. She'd been looking forward to cooking for Nick this weekend.

And while she was here in the Lakes, she wanted to find good, local food for their other meals.

'I'm just not sure what the kitchen is like,' Nick said. Laura thought he looked rather guilty.

'What do you mean?' she asked.

'It's just that the kitchen may not be very modern,' replied Nick. 'Anyway I want to buy you dinner. You've been working all week. You've earned it.'

The pub where they stopped for food was warm and welcoming, though it was almost empty.

Laura and Nick sat in a corner near the fire. There were flowers on their table. The pub smelt of wood smoke and good food. They studied the menu and chose their meals.

'Not bad,' said Laura, eating a piece of chicken pie and salad. She enjoyed tasting local food everywhere she went. She was always keeping an eye open for new things to sell in her café. Nick was eating pheasant.

'It's good that it's organic, local food, don't you think?' said Laura.

'Yeah, but I could do with a good Thai green curry,' said Nick, and Laura hit him playfully.

Kip sat under the table. Laura fed him bits of chicken.

At the bar sat a tall man with untidy fair hair. Laura looked at him. He was interesting-looking, she thought, with an intelligent face. But he looked sad.

What would Jo say about him? A poet, she might guess. A hill-walking poet, like Wordsworth?

The man didn't look at the couple, although they were the only other people in the room. If anything, Laura noticed, he seemed to turn away from them.

'They aren't very friendly around here,' said Nick. 'I thought Northerners were always friendly.'

'Well, it's just one person,' said Laura. 'You can't make up your mind about all Northerners because of one person's behaviour.'

'But there's nobody else here. Why doesn't he say hello?'

'Maybe he doesn't like tourists,' said Laura, beginning to build up a picture of the man in her head. She could see him walking across the hills in the rain, then going home to a tiny house and writing sad poems by the light of a fire. He was probably quite poor. Writers never earned much money.

'Do you think he's a poet?' she asked Nick.

'Who?' asked Nick.

'That man at the bar,' said Laura.

'A poet? I've no idea,' said Nick. 'He looks very unfriendly. That's all I can see. Why do you ask?'

'Oh, never mind,' said Laura. 'Look, I'm tired,' she said. 'Shall we get to the house?'

'House?' repeated Nick.

'The place where we're staying,' said Laura.

'Oh, that! Yes, let's go,' replied Nick.

Chapter 4 *Poison!*

'A barn? A farm building?' asked Laura.

'Yes, a barn!' replied Nick.

'But … But I thought you were a hot-bath and soft-towels sort of a man,' said Laura.

'Yes, I am, when I'm in London,' replied Nick. 'But when I'm in the country I like to live the country way.'

'Are you saying that country people all live in cold barns?' asked Laura, laughing.

'I'm saying that it's good for a man to give up his comfortable city life sometimes.'

'It may be good for men,' said Laura, 'but I'm not so sure it's good for this woman, or this poor little dog!'

They'd parked the car outside the door of a large, stone building. It was eleven o'clock at night and Laura couldn't believe her eyes as they pushed open the door. They might just as well be camping! There were lights, but not much else. No heating. No TV. No bath. There was a tiny kitchen with a camping stove to cook on. And at the top of some wooden stairs there were beds. It was cold.

Kip ran off across the big room into a smaller side room. Laura went into the kitchen.

'Nick, why didn't you tell me we were staying in a barn?' asked Laura.

'Because,' he said, putting his arms around her, 'I was afraid, if I told you, that you wouldn't come.'

'Well, you were right!' said Laura.

Nick laughed. 'But you're here now,' he said, 'and it's a long way home.'

Laura laughed too and let him pull her towards him. 'So you tricked me,' she said, 'into coming with you.'

'And you tricked me into bringing a dog with us,' he replied.

'Yes,' she said, smiling. He kissed her.

'I'd better just check on Kip,' said Laura.

Nick pretended to look hurt. 'I hope you don't start liking that dog more than you like me!' he said.

'Hey!' said Laura. 'You're not a helpless motherless animal! I'll just go and see …'

'You'll need a torch,' said Nick. 'There's no electricity in that room. Here you are.'

Laura went across the cold barn. She was surprised that Nick had chosen this barn for the holiday. He didn't seem like the kind of man to enjoy camping – it was interesting what people showed about themselves, the more you got to know them. But she felt happy. It showed he was even more interesting than she'd thought. And although she'd joked with Nick, Laura did in fact love camping. She loved the idea of cooking on a camping stove. She loved sitting by a real fire to keep warm! 'I'm a country girl at heart,' she thought. 'So, Nick and I are more alike than I imagined!'

She pulled her wool jacket around herself and went towards the side room holding the torch. She opened the door and shone the torch around the room. No Kip!

There was a door to the garden. Laura realised it wasn't shut properly. Had Kip gone out? She pushed the door open.

'Kip! Kip!' she called. She went outside and shone her torch about. It lit up the bushes and trees.

Laura's heart began to beat fast. She walked further out into the trees.

'Kip! Kip! Where are you?' she called. She began to feel worried. Perhaps he was lost. Perhaps a bigger animal had eaten him. Did foxes eat dogs? She had no idea.

What had happened to Kip? What would she do if she'd lost him? If Joseph knew something bad had happened to Kip, he'd be heartbroken and might not get better! She knew how much he loved his little dog.

She stood in the trees for several minutes calling, 'Kip! Kip!' but there was no sound.

'I'd better go back,' thought Laura. 'Nick will wonder where I am.' She turned back towards the barn.

'Laura! Laura! Where are you?' Nick was calling her.

'Out here. Looking for Kip,' she called back.

'He's here!' shouted Nick.

Laura moved as quickly as she could back through the trees. Nick stood by the door holding another torch.

'He was under the chair,' he said as Laura got back, 'but I think there may be something wrong with him.'

Laura bent down and touched the little dog. He didn't move or open his eyes.

'Hey, look! What's this?' asked Nick. His light was shining on some powder in an open box on the floor.

'What is it?' asked Laura, picking up the box.

Her heart jumped. On the box it said, 'Rat Poison'.

'Oh no! Nick, has he eaten it?' cried Laura.

'It looks like he's got the powder round his mouth,' replied Nick.

'Oh! What shall we do?' cried Laura.

'There isn't much we can do,' said Nick.

'I promised Joseph. I *promised* Joseph I would take care of him. Will he die, Nick?' said Laura.

'I've no idea,' said Nick.

'But if Kip dies, Joseph might die ... Look, we need to get him to a vet,' said Laura.

'Laura, it's nearly midnight!' said Nick.

'There must be emergency vets, like there are emergency doctors,' said Laura.

She was holding Kip on her knees. He looked very ill.

'Laura,' said Nick, 'we've only got four nights here alone together. I'm not spending one of them looking for a vet for an animal that isn't even ours!'

'I mustn't disappoint Joseph,' said Laura. She put her hand on the dog's side again. He felt cool.

'He's terribly ill,' she said, really frightened now. 'And it's my fault. We must do something!'

Laura looked at Nick. Why didn't he understand that she didn't *want* to do this, she *had* to? She had to do it because she'd promised Joseph.

Nick looked annoyed. 'I'm going to bed,' he said. 'I'm tired after the drive and I want to get up early tomorrow.'

Nick went upstairs, leaving Laura alone with Kip in her arms. She was near to tears. But were they tears of worry for the dog or disappointment with Nick? She wasn't sure.

Chapter 5 *Emergency call-out*

Another crash. A scream. Lights going on and off. Blood on the water.

Robert woke up. His heart was beating wildly, but the house was dark. It was the dream again. The same dream every night. The dream was like living that terrible night over and over again. Yet it was two whole years ago now. Why wouldn't it stop?

He sat up and looked at the clock. Midnight. After a few seconds, he realised the phone was ringing. He picked it up.

'Emergency. A poisoned dog,' a voice said. It was his emergency phone centre.

Robert wrote down a name, still half asleep. He put on his trousers and a big pullover, and set off to the surgery.

Often, the emergency calls came from people with pets that had nothing wrong with them, like Mrs Fellows' cat. Robert liked animals. But animals had different needs to people. They didn't need a vet every time they had a cold.

The worst people, Robert thought as he drove along, were the city people who came for holidays in the summer. They came with their ugly, bright-coloured clothes, and filled the lakes with their noisy water sports. Often, they brought dogs or even cats with them. Sometimes the dogs ran after the sheep on the hills. Farmers got angry about that.

But the real reason Robert disliked people from the city was more painful and he refused to talk about it.

There were no other cars on the road. He tried not to think of that evening two years ago as he drove. He needed to stay calm.

It took him ten minutes to get to his surgery. He jumped out of the car, opened the surgery door and put on the lights. He put some clean paper on the table and got some things ready. A poisoned dog. That was all he knew.

*　*　*

Laura didn't like driving alone along the dark roads at this time of night. But although she'd asked Nick again if he would come with her, he'd refused.

'Take the car if you like,' he'd said, 'but I need my sleep. It's up to you. You can stay here with me or take the dog to the vet. But I'm not going anywhere.'

She felt afraid as she drove along the empty, dark country roads, past the lake, then through some woods and up another hill, following – she hoped – the directions she'd been given on the phone.

She wished Nick was with her. She'd felt disappointed with him earlier, but now she thought about it differently as she drove.

'He said he didn't usually bring anyone to the Lakes with him,' she thought. 'He certainly didn't expect me to bring a dog. He doesn't want to spend all night looking for a vet. It isn't really surprising.'

It was nearly one o'clock when she stopped outside a small building. 'Veterinary Surgery' was written clearly above it. A light shone from inside, so she knew this must be the right place.

Kip was on the front seat of the car, covered with her jumper and coat to keep him warm. Laura lifted his little body out of the car, hurried to the door and rang the doorbell. The door opened.

Laura wasn't sure what she'd been expecting. Probably someone middle-aged, with grey hair and glasses. Instead, she recognised at once the man who'd been in the pub earlier that evening and thought, stupidly, 'But you're the poet!'

He was dressed in an old jumper and his fair hair was unbrushed. So, a vet, not a poet! Her guess had been very wide of the mark! If Kip hadn't been so ill, she might have smiled.

'You think he's been poisoned?' the vet asked, taking Kip from Laura.

'Yes, there was rat poison on the floor in the room where I left him,' said Laura.

'Did you bring some with you?' the vet asked.

'No,' replied Laura.

'And you didn't check the room before you left the dog in it?' the vet asked.

'No. We'd just arrived. It was a six-hour drive from London. I was tired, I didn't think … I didn't think there would be rat poison on the floor,' said Laura.

'Where are you staying?' the vet asked.

'We're camping …' Laura told him.

'You're camping?' the vet said.

'Well, it's sort of camping – in a barn,' explained Laura.

'Camping in a barn?' the vet said.

Laura wished he wouldn't keep repeating everything she said. It made her feel so stupid. And he still hadn't smiled.

His hair covered most of his face anyway, so she had no idea what he was thinking.

He was silent then, for what seemed like a long, long time.

Robert didn't speak. He felt annoyed. 'This is what they're like,' he thought. 'The people who come to the Lakes have no idea how to live in the country. You stay in a barn – so you don't want rats. Of course there'll be rat poison, and if you've got a dog, you check the place first.'

Laura watched. His big hands felt the dog's little chest, its tummy and picked up each of its ears in turn. He smelled the ears.

'Where is this place you're staying?' he asked.

'It's up on Bakestall Fell. It's like a … well, it's just a barn with some beds. It's pretty cold and there are obviously rats, but …' She realised he wasn't really listening.

'I need to give the dog some medicine,' he said.

'Will he be all right?' asked Laura.

'I think we're probably just in time,' the vet replied. He gave her a quick look. 'You were right to phone me. He could have died.'

While the vet gave the dog the medicine, Laura sat and watched. 'Why didn't I check the barn for poison?' she thought. 'But I'm not used to having a dog. I didn't think about Kip's safety.'

She watched the vet, his large hands working so gently on the dog. His face, although unsmiling, was a gentle face, she thought. But she noticed again that there was something deeply sad about him.

Kip's eyes were open now, and he looked a little better.

'It's a barn, you say. Is there any heating? Any hot water?' the vet asked.

'No, it's very basic,' Laura replied.

'Then, look,' he said. At last he stood up straight and looked at her, pushing the hair away from his eyes, which, she saw now, were blue. 'I'll take the dog back to my place tonight. It'll be better for him to be warm.'

Laura was surprised. Surprised and so thankful she wanted to kiss him. It seemed so kind – kinder than was necessary. But she could see that he wasn't the type of man you could kiss, however thankful you felt.

'Thank you,' she said instead. 'Thank you so much. You must think I'm stupid not checking the barn first, but …'

'I'll bring him back to you tomorrow. What's the address?' the vet asked.

Laura told the vet where the barn was and he nodded.

'I know it,' he said. 'I'm going out there anyway tomorrow to see a farmer. I'll bring the dog back in the morning, if he's better.'

'That's so good of you,' replied Laura. 'I feel so much better. I was worried and I didn't know what to do.'

Laura felt happy at last. Kip was going to be all right. She turned to go.

'Um …' The vet spoke just as she stepped out of the door. She turned round.

'I forgot to ask – what's his name?' the vet said.

'Whose name?' asked Laura.

The vet looked at her as if she was mad, then touched the dog's head.

'Oh … oh sorry,' said Laura. 'It's Kip.'

'Right. Good night,' he said.

And Laura set off again through the night feeling much better than she'd felt on the way there.

Chapter 6 *On the lake*

In the morning Nick came into the kitchen. Laura was cooking bacon on the tiny camping stove.

'That smells good,' he said.

'Here.' Laura handed him a plate. 'Perhaps we can go for a walk together before Nick goes off to do his water sports,' she was thinking.

Nick had other ideas. He ate his breakfast quickly, before Laura sat down.

'Right!' he said loudly. 'I feel better for that. Now, let's get going!'

'Already?' Laura asked.

'I don't want to waste any time,' said Nick. 'It's a beautiful morning and I want to get out on the lake while it's fine. Are you coming?'

'I'm … I'm not sure. What water sports are you doing? I quite like sailing, but I don't know if …'

'Jet-skiing,' said Nick.

'Jet-skiing?' Laura looked at him. Why was she surprised? Nick liked fast vehicles. He liked motorbikes and sports cars, so of course he liked jet-skiing.

'Coming?' he asked.

'No, no, I don't think so. I've never jet-skied. To be honest, I'm a bit afraid of it. You have to go so fast.'

'That's the fun!' said Nick. 'But don't worry. I'm happy to go on my own, and I can meet you back here for lunch.'

'OK. I'll come with you down to the lake, and walk back. I need some exercise too,' said Laura.

Nick hadn't asked about Kip. He'd been asleep when Laura had got back last night. Had he forgotten that she'd gone to the vet's in the middle of the night?

'The vet kept the dog overnight,' Laura said as they drove. 'He was worried he'd be cold in the barn.'

'That was kind of him,' said Nick. 'So, he was all right?'

'Yes, he was OK, a bit quiet,' replied Laura.

'No, I meant the dog,' said Nick laughing.

'Oh! Oh yes, Kip was OK. But it was lucky I went. The vet said he nearly died.'

'Hey, just look at that,' said Nick, not answering Laura. A bright yellow jet-ski was racing over the water, the sun behind it. 'That's going to be me soon!'

'Cool,' said Laura, suddenly realising how little interest she really had in jet-skis.

As they drove down the little roads – the same ones she'd gone down late last night – she thought how beautiful the countryside was. Tall hills rose on either side, lovely purple and red colours in the September sunshine, and the road turned towards the sheet of silver water that was the lake. Laura couldn't help thinking that the jet-skis on the lake were the only things that weren't beautiful.

At the water sports centre, Nick jumped out of the car and went to talk to someone.

Laura sat wondering why she was there. It was almost as if Nick had forgotten her now he was about to do the thing he loved so much – get onto a jet-ski. But to be fair, he'd told her he didn't usually invite his girlfriends. Perhaps this was why. He knew he would be busy.

'I'll just have to do things that I enjoy,' she thought.

'See you at lunchtime,' Nick said, coming back to the car.

'OK,' she said. 'I'll make lunch for you. I'll see you later.'

She didn't know why she felt disappointed. What had she expected? That they would spend the whole weekend sitting in cafés being romantic?

'No,' she thought. 'I knew it wouldn't be like that. But it would be nice to spend some time walking together. It's such a beautiful morning.'

She walked back along the quiet roads, thinking that this was the second time she'd gone along them alone since they'd arrived.

The fields were full of mushrooms, white in the morning light. She thought about picking some to make a really good mushroom omelette for lunch.

She went back to the barn, got a large bowl and set off up the nearest hill, picking mushrooms. She could listen out for the vet's car if she stayed near the barn.

'I hope Kip's all right,' she thought. 'I'll feel happier when he's back with me again.'

The smell of the countryside and the fresh air reminded her of being a child. She'd grown up in the countryside and often missed it. However, there just weren't the same opportunities in the country as there were in London. Her shop and café were going well and she couldn't leave them now.

'I wonder if I could be happy living somewhere like this again?' she thought as she walked.

Then she realised that something wasn't right. The peace of the countryside was being broken. It was the annoying sound of jet-skis going round and round out on the lake.

* * *

Maggie, the vet's receptionist, was sitting by her desk, looking in a small mirror and checking her make-up.

'Oh, what a little darling!' she cried, seeing the dog in Robert's arms.

'Ah, he's lovely! Whose is it? Who's your lucky mummy?' she asked, putting her hand on Kip's head. She looked up at Robert then.

'Are you coming to the White Bull later?' she asked him.

'Sorry, Maggie,' said Robert.

She smiled sweetly at him, hoping he would notice her long eyelashes.

'You need to get out more, you know,' she said. 'You're getting boring. You'll become a boring old man if you're not careful.'

Robert looked at his receptionist and gave her a quick smile. She was kind, she really was. And attractive. And she knew it! But he didn't want to spend an evening with Maggie while she talked about every pet that came into the surgery. She said he was getting boring, but she wasn't the most interesting company herself.

'I'm going out now,' he told Maggie. 'I've got to look at some cows up at Farmer Ainsworth's and I'll take this dog back to its owner on the way.'

Robert climbed into his Land Rover. He looked down at Kip on the seat beside him. He had to admit he quite liked this type of dog. Since Chiara had gone, he often felt lonely, but there was no way he could begin to share his life with another person. It would be too painful. Perhaps a dog instead? He thought about the farms around here. They didn't need more dogs running about, worrying the sheep.

The thoughts ran around his head as he drove towards the barn.

Kip had his front feet up against the window and was looking out. Suddenly he saw a rabbit in a field and jumped up and down, barking loudly. No, it would be difficult having a dog with him while he tried to work.

As Robert arrived at the barn, he saw that there was no car there. 'I don't believe it! She's gone out! She expects me to leave the dog in an empty barn,' he thought.

He got out of the Land Rover and shut the door. He walked up to the door of the barn. As he thought, it was locked. There was nobody in.

'I told that woman I'd come today,' he thought. 'Where is she? She didn't seem like the kind of woman to just forget about her dog. She seemed so worried about it!'

He walked once more around the barn, just to make sure there was nobody there. Then he remembered she said they'd come from London. He felt so annoyed he began to shake.

'She probably leaves the poor dog on its own every day in a small flat while she goes out to work,' he thought. 'It's normal for her to do this! She just has a dog because it's fashionable.'

For some reason, he felt disappointed as well as annoyed with the woman. He turned the Land Rover round and drove back down the road, with Kip still beside him.

'I'll go to Farmer Ainsworth's and come back later,' he thought.

He saw the yellow sports car as he was about to drive onto the main road. He recognised it as the car the woman had driven last night. It was parked beside the lake. And out on the lake he could see jet-skiers racing round and round, making silver patterns on the water. The skiers hadn't seen him. It would be impossible to hear a car, with all that noise. They were racing over the water, then turning suddenly so that they jumped into the air. Robert felt anger, anger that was almost like a pain in his body.

He realised one of the jet-skiers must be the owner of the car. So Kip's owner was out there jet-skiing instead of waiting at the barn for her dog! He felt the strange disappointment again.

'What sort of woman is more interested in jet-skiing than her own dog's health?' he thought.

He set off towards Farmer Ainsworth's still feeling angry. Why were jet-skiers still allowed on the lake? Nothing made him more angry and unhappy than the danger these people brought to the Lakes.

Chapter 7   *Angry words*

Laura collected enough mushrooms to make a good omelette. There were blackberries in the field as well and she picked some of these too. Back at the barn, she made a salad, cut up some ham and salami, and opened a jar of olives.

She put plates and glasses on the table ready for Nick when he returned from his jet-skiing.

She looked at her watch. It was nearly two o'clock! Laura couldn't believe it. Hadn't the vet said he would bring Kip back this morning?

Laura began to feel worried again. What if Kip hadn't got better after all? What if the poison had really hurt him?

When she heard the sound of a car coming, she hurried outside to see if it was the vet. She walked towards the gate and saw that it was Nick, racing up in the sports car.

He jumped out. 'That was wonderful!' he said. 'And I'm so hungry. Look, honey, I want to go water-skiing this afternoon. I met a man down there with a boat and skis, so I'll just eat a quick lunch and then I'll go. Are you OK?'

'I'm fine,' said Laura showing him the lunch she'd made. 'But I don't know where Kip is. The vet said he'd bring him back this morning. I hope he's all right.'

Nick sat and ate the food that was on the table. Then, with his mouth full, he went towards the door.

'Hey!' said Laura. 'I'm making an omelette …'

'An omelette?' Nick said. 'It's OK. I don't want anything else now. I'll be back about six o'clock. We can go back to that pub for supper. You don't need to cook.'

He stopped outside the door and walked back inside to Laura.

'Hey!' he said. 'Give us a kiss.'

Laura stood at the door and watched him disappear again in the sports car.

She turned back to the table, which was covered with good things to eat. She looked at the pile of mushrooms all ready to go in the omelette.

'What am I going to do with all this food?' she wondered. 'And what shall I do with the rest of the afternoon? What's happened to Kip?'

Feeling really unhappy now, she went and found her mobile and called the vet's number. Her heart was beating fast. But the vet's phone was on voice mail.

'It's Laura Barton here,' she said. 'You've got my dog, Kip. How is he? I was worried because you didn't come this morning. Can you phone me when you get this message?' She left her mobile number.

Feeling lonely, sad and worried about Kip, Laura got a book and went to sit outside in the sunshine. But she couldn't think about the story. And after about ten minutes the sky went dark and it began to rain. The rain was very heavy, as if the sky had opened.

'Am I going to spend the afternoon in this cold barn on my own?' she wondered. 'Surely Nick will come back, now it's raining?'

*   *   *

Nick had been water-skiing for about an hour, but the weather had got so bad he could no longer see through the rain.

'I think we'd better give up,' his friend shouted, turning off the boat's engine and helping Nick climb onto the boat. They went back to the beach.

Nick was pulling off his wetsuit when he noticed the Land Rover arriving. It stopped beside his car and a man jumped out. Nick recognised the tall man who had been in the pub on their first evening. He had Kip with him.

'Do you know where this dog's owner is?' the man asked.

'Laura? Hi, I'm her boyfriend,' said Nick, holding out his hand to shake the other man's. 'How do you do? I'm Nick.'

'Here's your dog,' said the vet. 'Perhaps you'd like him back now?'

Nick laughed. 'It's not my dog! It's Laura's.'

'Ah. Well, where is she? I need to give him back to her,' said the vet.

'She's up at the barn, as far as I know,' said Nick. 'Could you take the dog up to her? I've got to get changed and pack up my things.'

Robert decided not to argue. He didn't like the way this man spoke to him, but he wasn't surprised. He'd met people like Nick before. People who came from London and behaved as if they were more important than everyone else.

Robert turned his Land Rover round and set off for the barn again. He had more work to do this afternoon, and he needed to give this dog back. Once he'd returned Kip, he wouldn't have to have anything more to do with these two awful people.

He looked at Kip. He was a nice little dog, and Robert was sorry in a way to be giving him back.

'I'm sorry you have to live with owners like that,' he said to Kip, as he drove towards the barn. 'They clearly don't know how to look after you properly.'

* * *

Laura was in the barn cooking the blackberries. It was quite nice with the rain coming down. She tried to stop worrying about Kip. Then she heard the sound of a car engine again.

She looked out of the window through the rain. It wasn't the sports car this time. It was a Land Rover – it must be the vet at last. She went to the door.

The vet stood there in a long raincoat, holding Kip. He handed Laura the dog.

Laura took Kip in her arms, feeling a new love for the little dog now she had nearly lost him.

'Is he all right?' asked Laura. 'I've been so worried.'

'He's fine … now,' said the vet. 'I hope you've checked the barn for more poison?'

'Yes, I have,' said Laura, feeling like a small schoolchild.

'I'm a busy man,' said the vet. 'I don't need unnecessary emergencies.'

'No, I understand that,' replied Laura.

'He's a country dog,' the vet said then. 'You shouldn't leave him alone in a flat all day.'

Laura looked at the vet. Why did he sound so annoyed with her? He knew nothing about her.

'I know that,' she said. She looked at him again, but she suddenly felt she couldn't speak any more, even though there was so much to say.

She wanted to tell him that Kip belonged to an old man who loved him. An old man who was at home all day. She wanted to say so much, but she couldn't. She didn't know why.

'How much do I owe you?' she asked instead.

'That'll be a hundred pounds, please,' the vet replied.

Her heart began to jump again. She didn't have a hundred pounds! Or at least she didn't have a hundred pounds to spend on the dog.

'Do I … do I have to pay now?' she asked, feeling more stupid than ever.

The vet looked at her and for a moment Laura felt afraid that he was really angry. Then he surprised her, as he had done the night before.

'It's OK,' he said. 'Perhaps you could bring the money over to the surgery when you're passing.' He turned to leave. He'd noticed the lovely smell of blackberries cooking, coming from the kitchen, and it brought up memories for him he didn't want to think about.

'I'll bring the money to you tomorrow,' Laura said. 'I'm sorry … for the trouble.'

Laura felt again that she wanted to say more. She wanted to have a chance to explain herself. But at that moment Nick arrived in the sports car.

'What's going on?' he asked.

'I'm just arranging to pay the vet's bill,' said Laura. 'He's saved Kip's life!'

'How much money does he want?' asked Nick, as if the vet wasn't there.

'It's a hundred pounds,' said Laura. 'But it's OK. I'm going to pay him tomorrow after I've been into town.'

'A hundred pounds! Is that dog worth that much?' asked Nick.

The vet looked at Nick angrily. 'You wouldn't *be* spending a lot of money on him if you'd checked the barn for rat poison to begin with,' he said.

'We didn't expect there to *be* rat poison. What kind of a place uses rat poison?' asked Nick.

'Places where people don't want rats,' said the vet.

'But it's so old-fashioned! It's like going back a century round here!' said Nick and he laughed. The vet didn't even smile.

'Look,' said Laura. 'We made a mistake. You're right. We'll be careful in future. I'm going into town tomorrow. I'll get the money then. And,' she added, knowing it was always best to be polite in this kind of situation, 'thanks for saving Kip's life. I don't know what I'd have told Joseph if you hadn't.'

As the vet turned to leave he looked at Laura. He wondered who Joseph was. But he'd had enough of these two, so he drove away without asking.

Chapter 8 *A terrible accident*

Laura and Nick sat in the pub, eating supper.

'That's a nice little dog you've got there,' a voice said.

Laura looked up. The woman who was speaking to her was small and dark with shining blue eyes.

'Oh,' the woman said then, 'wasn't he at the vet's this morning?'

'Yes,' said Laura. 'How did you know?'

'Oh, I work there,' she said. 'I'm Maggie. I'm the vet's receptionist. I love animals. I've always loved them. Oh, look at him!'

'Ah,' said Nick. 'Then perhaps you can tell us why your vet's so rude?'

'Oh, he's not rude,' said Maggie. 'He's just sad. And if you knew what happened two years ago you'd understand why. He's hardly spoken to anyone since. Especially you city people. He's got no time for you.'

'Why's that?' Laura asked. She felt hurt, she realised, that Robert hadn't given her a chance just because she came from London.

'Well …' began Maggie. 'Do you mind?' she added, pulling up a chair.

'It's like this. Robert was going to be married to Chiara. She was Italian. She was a lovely girl – beautiful, kind *and* clever. She was training to be a doctor. Imagine! A vet and a doctor! So one evening she decides to go for a swim in the lake. It's a beautiful evening in early summer and it's still light. She and Robert quite often went swimming after work. But on this evening, Robert's working late, so he tells her he'll see her at the lake a bit later and she goes ahead on her own. There are some boys up from London, and they're messing about near the lake, talking about jet-skiing. There are quite a few people around, walking by the water, enjoying the evening.

'Chiara goes into the water and swims out. They say she swam along the golden path the sun made on the water as it went down. As I said, it was a beautiful evening.'

Maggie stopped and looked dreamily up at the ceiling for a minute. Then she went on.

'While she's out there, enjoying the sunset, the boys on the lake-side decide to go out on their jet-skis. The sun's quite low by now and possibly it's shining in their eyes ...'

Maggie stopped and had some of her drink. She was enjoying telling this story, it was clear, and Laura and Nick were a good audience.

'... or perhaps they're drunk because, somehow, they don't see Chiara. They're going really fast and shouting and making a lot of noise. Suddenly ... Bam! They hit her.'

Laura covered her ears. She didn't want to hear any more of this story. But Maggie wouldn't stop.

'They say she flew right up into the air. People say that for a few seconds she looked like a big bird, taking off from the water, but when she came back down, she was dead.'

Maggie looked up at Laura and Nick. Laura looked terrible. There were tears in her eyes. Nick looked annoyed.

'There's blood all over the water. And the boys on their jet-skis, they just disappear. The next day they've gone. Back to London. And nobody ever catches them.'

There was a few seconds' silence.

'That's terrible,' said Laura.

'Yes, and even more terrible, Robert arrived at the lake just in time to see Chiara die. He saw it all. He heard the sound of the jet-ski hitting her body, and saw her fly up into the air.

'Robert has had nothing to do with city people since then. And he's been trying to stop jet-skis on the lakes. He says they're not just dangerous, they're bad for the countryside and the wildlife. And some say he'll never get over Chiara's death and he'll live the rest of his life on his own. But that's only if I don't get my way!' she said laughing. 'He's really good-looking, don't you think so?' She looked at Laura as she said this and Laura felt herself go red.

*   *   *

It was Saturday morning. Laura made coffee on the tiny camping stove and took it up to Nick.

'Thanks, honey,' Nick said, taking the cup from her.

'Nick,' said Laura. She'd decided she needed to talk to him. She needed to know if she was going to spend any time with him at all this weekend.

'What are we going to do today? I thought perhaps we could go for a walk together. I don't feel I've seen you much since we got here. And there's a lovely hill we could walk up right behind the barn. There must be wonderful views from the top.'

'I tell you what,' said Nick. 'Why don't you come with me today? I could teach you how to jet-ski.'

Laura looked at him. His eyes were shining like the first time she'd seen him. It had been easy to like him then, when he first looked at her like this. Now, for some reason she didn't understand, it had no effect on her.

'I'm not sure,' she said. 'I don't think I'd be very happy jet-skiing after what that woman told us in the pub last night.'

'Oh, you don't want to worry about stories like that,' said Nick. 'These locals get very angry about tourists. They forget that actually we bring in a lot of money.'

'But don't you think she's got a good argument?' asked Laura.

'A good argument about what?' replied Nick.

'About stopping jet-skiing?' continued Laura.

'She wasn't suggesting stopping jet-skiing,' said Nick.

'OK, she wasn't suggesting it herself. She was telling us what the vet thinks,' said Laura.

'Was she? I thought she was just telling us that he can't get over his girlfriend's death. He needs to accept it and move on. He can't expect everyone to give up their sports just because of one accident,' said Nick.

'But the point was that his girlfriend was killed by jet-skiers. Don't you think that's terrible?' asked Laura.

'Laura, I can jet-ski if I choose to. If that man's got a problem with it, he should either live somewhere else or shut up about it,' said Nick. He got out of bed.

'I'd *like* you to come with me,' he said. 'You should be pleased. I don't usually invite my girlfriends jet-skiing with me.'

'I'm sorry, Nick. I can't. Not after hearing that story. And anyway I've got Kip to think about.'

'Kip! All you ever think about is that dog. Well, if you're not coming,' Nick said, 'I want to get out on the lake right now. We've only got two more days.'

Laura gave up. 'OK. Look, Nick, if you're going out all morning again, please can I have the car? I'm going to take Kip for a walk, but after that I need to go into town to get some money. Then I need to pay the vet.'

'Sure. Drop me off and you can have the car for as long as you like,' replied Nick.

Half an hour later Laura watched as Nick went noisily out across the lake, his jet-ski tearing into the peace of the morning. She thought of the story Maggie had told them last night. It was terrible!

'How could Nick go straight out there after such a story?' she wondered as she drove away from him. 'And I just can't understand why he wants to race over the lakes like that. For me the beauty of the Lake District is its peace. Why can't Nick understand that?'

Chapter 9   *Alone again*

Laura drove the car back up to the barn and found Kip. 'Let's walk,' she said. 'I need some air and exercise.'

She started walking up the hill behind the barn. It was a beautiful morning, the air washed clear by yesterday's rain. Soon they were high up, looking down on the countryside below. It was a wonderful view.

'Come on, Kip!' shouted Laura. 'Let's go right up to the top!' They climbed higher and higher until the lake looked tiny below them, and the jet-skis on it looked like flies.

When they got to the top, Laura found a rock to sit on. She took in big breaths of the sweet fresh air, and Kip sat beside her.

'This is so good for me!' Laura said to Kip. 'I really need space sometimes. It clears my mind. I wonder if I could live somewhere like this again.

'I love these mountains and the fields and the woods. I think my dream would be to run my café in a small town, and live somewhere beautiful like this. London is exciting, but it's so busy and noisy. I don't know if it's for me. And,' she said, looking down at Kip, 'if I lived somewhere like this, I could perhaps even get a little dog like you.'

She only began to think it was odd later, as she made her way back down the hill, that she hadn't included Nick in this dream life.

As she got to the road at the bottom of the hill, she saw a Land Rover coming towards her. Kip was running along ahead of her.

Laura's heart jumped. It was the vet! Was he going to tell her she shouldn't be walking on this side of the road? Tell her off for letting Kip run in the fields? Ask for the money from her again? Laura wished she could hide somewhere, but it was too late. The Land Rover came right up beside her and stopped, and Robert looked out of the window.

'How is he?' he asked, looking at Kip.

'He's fine. Much better,' said Laura. 'I'm bringing the money later today,' she said, before he could mention it. 'I'm going into town to do a bit of shopping. I'll get some money while I'm there.'

'Oh, OK,' said Robert.

There was a silence, so Laura began to talk. She felt nervous.

'I want to look at some of the local food shops. I thought perhaps they could help. I'm looking for a supplier from this area. I'd like to sell some food from round here in my shop.'

'Your shop?' he asked.

'It's a food shop with a café,' she found herself explaining. 'An organic food shop.'

'Oh,' he said again. He was looking at her with surprise. 'Actually, there's a very good organic food shop in Cockermouth. My aunt runs it. She gets her cheeses from the farms round here.'

'Really? That sounds great,' said Laura.

'And I can easily give you the names and addresses of some cheese suppliers when you bring the money later,' he said.

'Thanks!' said Laura and smiled at him. But he was already driving away.

* * *

Back at the surgery that afternoon, Robert jumped out of his Land Rover.

Maggie was waiting at the door. It had begun to rain and she was standing under an umbrella. Robert leant across her and opened the door with his key. Maggie looked up at him, hoping he might return her look, but as usual Robert didn't seem to notice her.

'What have we got this afternoon?' he asked, as she started up the computer.

She read off the list of people who had booked in their animals. There was a sheep he needed to visit, and a pony, later on when he did his rounds. But right now there was a woman arriving with a rabbit that wasn't eating, and another one with a big dog.

'Oh,' said Maggie. 'And I forgot to tell you, that woman – the one with the lovely little dog called Kip – she phoned yesterday morning and left a message. She wondered why you hadn't brought the dog back. She sounded worried.'

Robert looked at Maggie. 'Why didn't you tell me yesterday?' he said.

'I didn't think it mattered,' she replied. 'I knew you'd gone that way anyway.'

Robert said nothing and disappeared into his surgery.

Later that afternoon he was just saying goodbye to a girl with a cat when Maggie put her head round the door of his surgery. She handed Robert a cup of tea.

'That lady called Laura is here,' Maggie said. 'She's got that nice little dog with her. She's paid, but she says you've got something for her. A farmer's address or something.'

Robert put his tea down. 'Yes, I know what she wants,' he said to Maggie. 'Send her in.'

Laura came into the room. She was holding Kip under one arm and for a second Robert felt his heart quicken, a feeling he'd almost forgotten. It was to do with the little dog, he thought. Perhaps it was simply that he wished he was holding it instead of Laura.

'So he's OK now? No more problems?' asked Robert, resting his hand on Kip's head. His hand touched Laura's arm by mistake and she quickly moved away.

'He's fine. Thanks,' said Laura, surprised that the vet was asking her again. He'd already asked her if Kip was OK this morning.

She looked at the vet. He was looking at Kip very lovingly, Laura thought. Then she thought, 'No, that's crazy. The vet sees dogs all the time. Why would he like Kip any better than any of the other dogs he cares for?'

Maggie interrupted them. 'Mrs Pierce wants to see you with her Labrador,' she said to Robert. 'He's behaving badly, and she wants him to see a psychologist.'

'OK. Tell her I'll be with her in just one moment,' said Robert, and Maggie left the room.

Laura tried not to smile at the thought of a dog psychologist and she wondered if Robert was trying not to smile too.

He looked at Laura, and for a second their eyes met, before he looked away again.

'It sounds funny,' he said, as he copied an address onto a piece of paper. 'But I've got this idea that people often come to see me with their animals, not because the animal is sick, but because they need some help themselves.'

'Really? That's interesting,' said Laura, surprised that the vet was suddenly talking to her like this.

'Yes. This dog that behaves badly … It's actually the owner who is ill. She suffers badly from depression. She's the one who needs a psychologist, not the dog. Or perhaps,' he added, 'the dog needs a psychologist *because* the owner needs one.'

It was the longest sentence she'd ever heard him speak and Laura was surprised – surprised and interested in what he'd said.

'So do you tell the owners to go to a doctor? When you see that they're sick, I mean,' she asked him.

'That's not my job,' said Robert. 'I can listen, but it's not my job to tell them what to do.'

'I sometimes feel a bit like that in my café,' said Laura. 'People tell me all sorts of things, but I can't tell them what to do about it. Sometimes people just need to talk.'

'Exactly,' said Robert. 'Now, here are those addresses you wanted.'

'Thanks,' said Laura. 'I must go, and let you get on.'

Laura felt strange as she left the surgery. The vet had spoken more than he ever had before. And he'd spoken to her as if he knew she would understand what he was saying.

'I won't see him ever again now I've paid him,' she thought.

As she drove away she realised that this last thought made her feel sad.

'It's because I want to show him I'm not the hopeless Londoner he thinks I am,' she thought, trying to explain her feelings.

47

Chapter 10   *A birth*

Laura looked at the addresses on the paper the vet had given her. She took out a map. There was a farm that made and sold cheese quite near the barn. Yes, she could drive back to the barn and then walk to the farm with Kip.

Half an hour later Laura was walking towards the farm with Kip beside her. The farm was almost on the top of a hill. It was a hard walk across fields and up the hill, and the sky had clouded over again. It was going to rain.

Laura took Kip under one arm, and went to the farmhouse door and knocked. Some hens were running about in the farmyard.

Nobody came to the door. A cow was making a loud noise on the other side of the farmyard. It sounded as if it was in pain. Kip barked.

Laura knocked on the door again, then gave up and went across the farmyard towards the sound of the cow. Walking around a barn she saw a young man bent over a cow that was lying on its side. The man looked at her.

'She's having a baby,' he shouted, 'but the calf's got stuck. I've phoned the vet. I thought you were him.'

Laura didn't know what to do. 'I'm in the way,' she said. 'I wanted to ask about your cheese, but I'll come back another time.'

'You could help, actually,' said the man. 'Just until the vet arrives. If you could tie the dog up and hold the cow's head still.'

'Oh dear,' thought Laura. 'This is the last thing I expected.' She tied Kip's lead to a gate and went back to the farmer.

'Hold her head still and talk to her,' said the farmer. 'I'm going to have to tie a rope to the calf's leg. It's breech.'

Laura knew that breech meant the calf was coming out the wrong way round.

'It could be dangerous to the calf *and* its mother,' said the farmer.

The cow mooed loudly and painfully. Laura touched its nose gently. 'It's OK,' she said. 'It's going to be OK.'

'I'm going to need some help this end,' shouted the farmer. 'We need to get this calf out quickly.'

Laura began to feel frightened. She had never done anything like this before. She went round to the cow's tail end and helped the farmer pull on the rope.

'It's coming,' he said.

The cow let out a loud cry again and the farmer pulled. His face was wet with sweat. The cow mooed loudly again.

'No, it's stuck. We'll have to give up in a minute. I just hope the vet gets here soon.'

At the mention of the vet again, Laura's heart jumped. Or was it just the effort of helping the calf out?

'Let's have one more try,' said the farmer, and Laura pulled as hard as she could.

After several more minutes, at last the calf was born. The farmer held it until it let out a cry, then put it on the ground. It shook itself. The cow turned and touched it and within a few minutes the calf stood up on thin legs.

Laura looked at it. 'Amazing!' she said. 'There's something so amazing about seeing an animal being born.'

'Yes. Thank goodness!' the farmer said. 'I thought we'd lost them both. We were just in time.'

He turned to her. 'You weren't expecting this, were you? You came to ask about … What was it?'

'About cheese. I was … I was hoping you might let me taste your cheeses. I've got a shop in London and I'm looking for new suppliers. But perhaps this isn't a good time to ask.' Laura had untied Kip and was holding him again.

'No, it's fine. Cheese … Hmm. You'd better come into the house. If you don't mind waiting while I wash.'

Laura sat in the farmhouse kitchen and, when he'd washed, the farmer offered her some of his cheeses to taste.

'These are delicious. Really special,' said Laura. 'I'd definitely like to order some.'

'That's great!' said the farmer and he got out some paper to write down his email address.

'Oh goodness. Look at the time,' Laura said suddenly. 'I need to get Nick from the lake.'

'Nick?' asked the farmer.

'Yes. He's my boyfriend. He's jet-skiing,' Laura explained. 'I promised I'd be there by six so we could get to the pub early for a meal.'

She arranged to email the farmer when she got back to London, and set off across the fields with Kip running along beside her. She felt pleased with herself. The afternoon had turned out to be quite exciting, and she'd found some delicious cheese to sell.

Just as she disappeared into the trees, Robert's Land Rover pulled up at the farm.

'You're too late,' said the farmer, coming out of the house. 'The calf is born. And I think it's OK.'

'I'll check it over anyway,' said Robert. He knew this farmer well and each of his cows was special to him.

'I'm sorry it took me so long. There was another emergency at Top Farm. A horse with a broken leg.'

'Don't worry – I was lucky. A woman arrived just in time,' said the farmer. 'She helped me.'

'Oh?' said Robert.

'Yes. She'd come asking for cheese, for a shop she runs in London, but she ended up helping me instead. Quite an adventure for her.'

'Oh, that's good,' said Robert, realising that the farmer must be talking about Laura. 'So where is she now?'

'She had to go. To get her boyfriend from the lake so they could get to the White Bull early. Tourists obviously.'

'Yes,' said Robert. 'I think I've met them.'

'The worst sort,' said the farmer. 'Jet-skiers.'

'Well, *he* is. She doesn't seem to be interested,' said Robert. The farmer pulled a face, and Robert said no more.

After he'd checked the cow and calf, Robert drove back to the surgery, where Maggie was just clearing up.

'Thank goodness it's Saturday night, and I'm not on call,' he said.

Maggie, seeing that he was smiling, said, 'How about coming for a drink at the White Bull tonight?'

'Oh, OK,' Robert replied. And Maggie looked at him. She couldn't believe her luck.

'Did you just say yes?' she asked.

'Yes, I just said yes,' said Robert, and Maggie laughed and laughed.

Chapter 11 *Two couples*

Laura drove back to the lake and sat in the car. Nick was still out on the water and it had begun to rain hard. Kip sat beside her. They watched the rain come down, and the jet-skis out on the lake jumping across the water.

At last Nick came over. He threw his wetsuit into the car.

'Let's get straight to the pub. I'm ready to eat,' he said.

She was getting used to Nick's ways. He wasn't going to ask her what she would prefer to do. He made all the decisions and expected her to agree with them. They sat in silence as they drove.

After a few minutes, Laura felt uncomfortable with the silence.

'So, you had a good day?' she asked him.

'Great! You?' he answered.

'Yes. I went to find a cheese supplier for my shop, and ended up helping a cow give birth!'

'Good,' said Nick.

'Good?' Laura began to feel angry. Wasn't Nick even listening to her properly?

'No, Nick, it wasn't just good – it was amazing! Watching – *helping* a new life to begin. There's nothing like it. It made me think my life's quite dull.'

'What? Duller than a cow's?' Nick laughed.

'No, I mean duller than a vet's,' Laura replied.

'A vet's?' asked Nick.

'Yes. I mean that's a vet's job – helping animals to give birth. It's so important, so interesting and so moving,' said Laura.

'Was the vet there too?' asked Nick.

'No, it was just the farmer and me,' said Laura.

'Then the vet isn't doing a very good job, is he? He wasn't even there when he was needed. Now,' Nick said, taking her hand and smiling at her, 'what are we going to eat tonight?'

* * *

The pub was busier this evening.

'What are you going to have?' Nick asked Laura.

She looked at the menu for some time. She was finding it hard to decide. There were other thoughts going through her mind, making her feel unhappy and confused.

At last she said, 'I'll have the meat and vegetable pie. How about you?'

'Fish and chips,' he said. 'I've had enough of all this local food.'

'I'll order the food,' said Laura. 'And I'll get some drinks at the same time,' and she went to the bar.

* * *

Maggie and Robert were sitting on stools at the bar.

'Wasn't that Persian cat beautiful that came in this afternoon?' Maggie asked. 'It had the most amazing eyes!'

Robert smiled, but said nothing. Maggie was very sweet. But why did she only ever want to talk about animals – and usually the ones he was least interested in?

'You could do worse than get yourself a cat, you know,' Maggie went on. 'They're nice to have around and they take care of themselves.'

'Look, Maggie, I know you mean well, but I'm really not interested in getting a cat at the moment,' Robert said.

Maggie pulled a face, pretending to be hurt. 'Sorry,' she said. 'It's just, you know, I worry about you living all on your own.'

'Don't worry,' said Robert. 'It may be hard for you to understand, Maggie, but there are people who like living alone better than sharing their house with anyone – anyone with two legs or anyone with four.'

'But you're a vet!' said Maggie.

'It doesn't mean I want to *live* with cats. Animals have a place, yes,' explained Robert. 'I like helping them out, as you know. I especially like to help farmers, and I felt really bad this afternoon that I missed helping that calf being born.'

'Ugh!' said Maggie, making a face.

'What do you mean "Ugh"?' asked Robert.

'I don't know – the thought of, you know, pulling a calf out of a cow,' said Maggie.

'Helping animals to give birth is actually the best part of my job,' Robert said. 'It's more exciting than giving cats medicine for their colds. And seeing an animal being born is beautiful.'

'What's so beautiful?' An older woman had come across the bar to talk to them. She had white-grey hair and was smartly dressed in a silk jacket and skirt.

'Barbara!' said Robert, standing up and kissing her. 'How nice to see you. What are you doing here?'

'I'm having dinner,' she said, nodding towards a man at a table on the other side of the bar. 'Ian invited me.'

'That's great!' said Robert. 'Maggie, this is my aunt, Barbara. She runs a food shop in Cockermouth. Barbara, this is my receptionist, Maggie.'

'How do you do, Maggie?' said Barbara.

She looked at Robert and his receptionist. 'So,' she thought. 'At last. Robert is beginning to be sociable again. And it looks as if he's got himself a girlfriend.'

'We've had a busy day,' Robert began to explain. 'Maggie suggested a drink and ...' He stopped. He could feel something warm against his leg. He looked down and two brown eyes were looking up into his.

'Kip!' he said brightly.

'I'm so sorry.' Laura was hurrying towards them. 'He saw you and he just ran towards you,' Laura said to Robert. 'I couldn't stop him. He's clearly become very attached to you.'

Robert smiled at the dog, and then looked up at Laura.

'It's OK,' he said. 'Listen, it's good that you're here. This is my Aunt Barbara. She runs the shop in Cockermouth I told you about this morning. Barbara, this is Laura.'

'Oh!' said Laura. 'How nice to meet you. I run a food shop too, but in London.'

Barbara looked at Laura, then at Robert.

'So ... how do you know each other?' she asked. She knew Robert didn't like Londoners, and it seemed strange that he was being friendly to Laura.

'Oh, Robert saved Kip's life,' said Laura, pointing at her little dog.

'And you helped a cow give birth this afternoon,' Robert said suddenly. Laura looked at him.

'Yes,' she said. 'I ... I just happened to be there ... and, well, you weren't ...'

'You're taking my work away from me,' said Robert without smiling.

Laura looked at him and felt afraid again. Was he really angry with her?

Then he smiled. 'Don't look so worried,' he said. 'I was joking.'

'No, but he's right!' said Maggie, looking straight at Laura. 'It can be dangerous trying to help with animals when you know nothing about them. The calf could have died.'

'Oh!' said Laura. 'But it didn't. And anyway I didn't mean to help. The farmer asked me to. There was nobody else there. He was waiting for ... waiting for ...'

'He was waiting for me,' Robert said to Maggie. 'But I was with that horse, the one with the broken leg.'

'Well, I must get back to Ian now. If you'd like to visit my shop, I'd love to talk to you more,' Barbara said to Laura. 'I'll be in tomorrow morning, but I close at twelve. We always go for a good long walk on Sunday afternoons.'

'OK, I'd love to come,' said Laura. 'Thank you. It was very nice to meet you.'

As she walked back to Nick, Laura could feel Maggie's eyes watching her go.

Chapter 12   *A new friend*

Laura went back to Nick, while Kip stayed under Robert's feet. She tried not to think about Robert and Maggie sitting so comfortably together there, or the way Maggie had looked at her. She felt something, but didn't try to decide what it was. The good thing was that she was getting some new suppliers for her shop, and now she was going to visit that nice lady Barbara tomorrow. They could give each other ideas.

'Wow!' said Nick, as Laura sat down. 'Isn't that the woman we were talking to last night?'

'Yes,' said Laura. 'Why?'

'Well, she's lovely. I can't think why she's with that horrible vet.'

Laura looked back at the couple at the bar. She hadn't really looked at Maggie properly before.

'I suppose she is very pretty,' said Laura. 'But the vet is good-looking too, and he's quite nice really. They make a good couple.'

She was staring across the bar at the two people. Their heads were bent together as they chatted, and she wondered what they were talking about.

* * *

When Laura woke up the next morning, Nick had already gone out. There was a note in the kitchen. 'Out on the lake. Back at lunchtime,' it said.

Laura felt unhappy, but there was nothing she could do about it. She sat and looked at Kip.

'What's happening, Kip?' she asked the dog. 'Nick isn't the person I thought he was. And my guess is, I'm not the person he thought I was either. It's always the same! How do I do it? How do I always choose the wrong men?'

She thought again about their first night here. How she'd had to drive alone through the night to find the vet. It seemed that when Nick didn't want to do something he just didn't do it. And his ideas about the countryside here made her unhappy too, however much she tried to understand them.

'He doesn't really want me here,' she thought. 'I'm beginning to think he's just not right for me.'

Suddenly Laura remembered that Barbara had invited her to see her shop this morning, and she suddenly felt brighter.

'I've got my own life to live,' she thought. 'Who needs men anyway, eh Kip?'

She looked at her watch. It was quarter past ten now. It was probably half an hour's drive to Cockermouth. If she left now she would get there in plenty of time.

Luckily, Nick had left the car for her and she got in and set off to Cockermouth.

It was a beautiful morning. Yesterday's rain had made everything shine like glass in the morning sunshine and the colours were bright. She felt clear-headed now she had thought carefully about her relationship with Nick.

'I'm going to work hard at my business,' she thought, 'and learn what I can from Barbara. I'm not going to worry about relationships for now.'

Barbara's shop was at one end of the High Street. Laura parked the car and walked along the street with Kip. It was an interesting little town with some nice shops.

Laura found Barbara's shop and went in.

Barbara came out from the back of the shop, smiling warmly.

'Hello, my dear. How nice of you to come,' she said.

'Janie's looking after the shop for me, so we can talk. Come through to the back.'

Laura followed her, noticing the jars of interesting foods on sale.

'So,' Barbara said, several minutes later, 'tell me about your shop, how you started, what you sell and so on.'

The shop was at the front of a large house, and they were now sitting in the kitchen. Barbara gave Laura a glass of home-made lemonade.

Laura told Barbara all about her shop in London and they talked for ages, not noticing the time.

'You must taste these pies,' Barbara said, getting something out of the oven. 'A local woman makes them for me. They would go down well in your café. Robert loves this one.' She handed Laura a piece of delicious-looking pie.

'Robert?' asked Laura, biting into the pie.

'Yes. He loves my food,' said Barbara. 'What do you think of him? He can seem a bit unfriendly, but he's got a good heart. Do you know why he's so quiet?'

'I heard the terrible story about his girlfriend,' said Laura.

'Yes. It was an awful thing,' Barbara said. 'It's affected him very deeply.'

'Yes,' said Laura.

'It wasn't just her death,' said Barbara, 'it was the fact that nobody ever caught the people who killed her. Robert feels that while people are still allowed to use jet-skis on the lakes, another accident may happen.'

'Well, he's got a point,' said Laura.

'But he needs to move on,' said Barbara. 'It's not good to hold on to such a terrible memory. He needs to forget what happened and start to live a full life again.'

'It must be very hard for him,' said Laura, remembering the terrible description Maggie had given them in the pub. 'Anyway, isn't he seeing his receptionist these days?'

'Well, he was with her last night,' said Barbara. 'But she isn't his type, if you ask me. Anyway,' she went on, 'what do you think of the pies?'

'They're perfect!' said Laura, slowly taking in everything this woman was telling her. 'And you say Robert likes them too?'

'Oh, he likes all good food,' said Barbara. 'Or at least he used to. Before Chiara died he used to be a very good cook himself. Then he lost interest in everything after she died. Everything except his work, that is. He really cares about the farmers and their animals. He's a good man, he really is.'

'Yes. And I'm very thankful to him. For two things: introducing me to you and for saving Kip's life.' Laura touched Kip's head.

'He's a nice little dog. You must be very attached to him,' said Barbara.

'Oh, he's not mine,' replied Laura. 'I'm looking after him for the old man who lives next door to me – he had to go into hospital the day before we came up to the Lakes. I don't really want a dog myself, not in London where they don't get much exercise. But it's funny how you get attached when you're with them all day.'

'Yes, I'm sure you do,' said Barbara. She leant back and smiled at Laura. 'So have you enjoyed your holiday in the Lakes?'

'Oh yes, I love it here,' said Laura with feeling. 'I've always loved it. I came here as a child. I thought perhaps it had changed, but it's just as beautiful.'

'It's busier than it used to be. The lakes get very busy with people doing water sports.'

'Yes, that's changed. I came here with Nick, my boyfriend. He likes jet-skiing, but I'm not interested. I prefer walking. So Kip and I have been out walking by ourselves.'

'Oh, well, listen! Why don't you come with us this afternoon? I told you we go on a walk every Sunday after lunch. Would you like to join us? There are quite a few people coming and you'd be most welcome.'

'Oh, I'd love to,' said Laura.

'We're meeting at Coniston Lake at two o'clock. I'll look forward to seeing you later.'

Chapter 13   *On the walk*

'You went off without telling me where you were going!' Nick said crossly when Laura arrived back at the barn.

'I'm sorry, Nick. You went off without me, and I forgot to tell you I had to be in Cockermouth before twelve.'

'OK. Well I want to get back on the water, so let's go!'

'We haven't had any lunch,' said Laura.

'I had a sandwich while I was waiting for you,' said Nick. 'Really, Laura, I don't want to waste any more time. We're leaving tomorrow.'

'Nick, all you seem to think about is your water sports! I have to say that I'm finding it rather difficult to accept.'

Nick stopped on his way to the car with an armful of wetsuits and looked back at Laura.

'Are you? You knew this was why I was coming to the Lakes. It's why I usually come alone. I asked you to come because I *thought* you were the kind of woman who would understand.'

'I do understand, up to a point. But Nick, we've hardly had any time together,' said Laura.

'That's because you aren't interested in jet-skiing,' Nick replied.

'No, I'm not …' Laura started.

'And because you brought that stupid dog with you!' Nick went on.

'Nick, that's not true,' Laura said.

'You spent the first night driving round the countryside looking for that bad-tempered vet,' Nick said.

'That was one night! And Nick, I had no choice, I was doing it for Joseph,' Laura said.

'Exactly. You were putting an old man before me,' said Nick.

'Nick, the dog nearly died! But since then we've had three days here and we've spent no time together. You're always out on the lake!' said Laura.

'Then why don't you come with me? Perhaps you would enjoy it,' said Nick.

'No, I wouldn't enjoy it. Because I care about what the local people here think, and you don't,' said Laura.

'No, Laura, I don't care! If you think I'm going to stop doing the thing I enjoy most, you're wrong! I work 24/7 to earn enough money to live, and this is my big interest,' said Nick.

'It's just that I can't believe you don't care that a woman *died*,' said Laura.

'Yes, she died. It's not my fault she died. She was swimming in a lake while people were jet-skiing! That's why she died. If it was anyone's fault, it was her own!' said Nick.

'And jet-skis are so bad for the …' said Laura.

Nick had got into the car and was starting the engine angrily. Laura ran to the car.

'I'm sorry, Nick,' she said. 'I shouldn't say these things. I can't help it. I feel things so strongly sometimes and I can't just keep quiet about them.' Nick didn't answer. Laura got into the car next to him. 'Look Nick, if you're going jet-skiing again please can I have the car this afternoon? I've been invited on a walk and I'd really like to go.'

'A walk? Who with?' asked Nick.

'With a woman – the one I met in the pub last night. The one with the shop in Cockermouth.'

'Oh, OK. You can have the car,' said Nick, without looking at her.

*   *   *

That afternoon, Laura went back to meet Barbara and her friends. She was looking forward to walking with someone who knew the Lakes well.

As she drove she realised she felt sad. It wasn't working with Nick, and she already knew what would happen when they got back to London. Once they were back in their own lives it would be over. Laura thought of her flat and her job. Yes, they kept her busy. But how empty and pointless they seemed when there was nobody to share them with. It was so hard to find anyone who really understood what she was trying to achieve in her life.

She looked at Kip. 'No wonder some people just choose dogs for friends,' she said out loud. 'You're a lot less complicated.'

She arrived at the meeting place Barbara had told her about, and stood feeling a little shy. There were several older people there, wearing walking boots and carrying sticks. Suddenly Kip jumped to his feet and barked happily.

Laura looked up. Coming across the field from the village was Robert. Laura felt surprised. Robert arrived at the group and stood, silent, among them.

Barbara went over to Laura and whispered in her ear. 'I persuaded Robert to come,' she said. 'It's the first time he's agreed to a group walk for … well, for years. We should be pleased.'

They started walking along the bottom of the hills. Kip wanted to go to Robert and at last Laura let him take her to him.

'Hi,' she said.

'Barbara invited me for this walk,' he said, his head down, as if he was embarrassed. 'I don't usually enjoy being in a group – I prefer walking alone. But she wanted me to come and I gave in.'

They were walking along beside a stream, and the air smelt fresh and clean.

Soon they started to climb and the countryside fell away below them. Robert walked ahead, with Kip at his heels, so Laura began to walk beside Barbara. They chatted easily together about their shops.

'I've been hearing about Laura's shop and café,' Barbara told Robert later when they all stopped for a rest. 'It sounds lovely. We've already agreed my pies would sell very well there.'

'Good. That's excellent,' said Robert.

Kip came running over towards Robert again. 'That dog of hers seems to like you, Robert,' said Barbara. 'Well, it's not hers, of course, but …'

'What do you mean?' asked Robert.

'Oh, didn't she say? He belongs to an old man who had to go into hospital just before she came away. She's looking after it for him.'

'Oh!' said Robert, suddenly feeling everything fall into place. 'Oh, now I see.'

And he looked across the group at Laura. She was definitely different to what he had first thought. So the dog wasn't hers. She wasn't a terrible city type who kept a dog because it was fashionable, as he'd thought. 'Yet how can she go out with that awful man?' he wondered.

They continued to climb up the hill. Barbara turned round to wait for a friend, so Robert and Laura found themselves walking along side by side.

Robert nodded towards the woman Barbara was waiting for. 'She's called Mrs Fellows,' Robert said. 'She called me out one night because her cat was sneezing. The cat was fine, but *she* talked for half the night. Do you see what I mean?'

'You mean, she's the one who needed you, not the cat?'

'Yes,' answered Robert.

'Do you think everyone who brings an animal to see you has a problem of their own?' asked Laura.

'Not everyone, no,' Robert replied.

He looked sideways at her and Laura felt at last that he was warming to her.

'What about me?' Laura asked suddenly. 'That night I came to see you – did you think I needed help, not Kip?'

'Ah,' said Robert, smiling suddenly. 'Well, Kip did need help. Kip ate something that wasn't good for him. But perhaps you're doing something that isn't good for you! I think that could be true.'

'Like what?' asked Laura, laughing. She enjoyed this game. It reminded her of the one she played with Jo in the shop, guessing about people and what they did.

'Only you know that,' said Robert. Then he threw a stick for Kip and began to run after him, while Laura was left wondering, 'What does he mean?'

Chapter 14 *Robert's house*

Two hours later they arrived back at the bottom of the hills.

'That was a lovely walk,' said Laura to Barbara. 'Thank you so much for asking me along. I enjoyed it and so did Kip. I'd better get going now though. We're leaving tomorrow and I've got to pack.'

'Well, don't forget to phone or email me with your orders for the shop,' said Barbara. 'Or about anything else you may want. It's been a pleasure meeting you. Now then, Robert,' she said, turning to the vet, 'didn't you say you'd left the Land Rover at the garage and you needed a lift home?'

'I did,' said Robert.

'And Laura, you're staying over in Robert's direction, aren't you? You don't mind giving him a lift, do you?' asked Barbara.

Laura was afraid she was going to go red. She didn't know why.

'That's fine,' she said, letting her hair blow over her face.

'Thanks,' he said.

'And,' said Barbara, looking at Laura, 'I'll get the first order to you by mid-November.'

'If you don't mind, that would be great. In time for Christmas.' Laura looked into Barbara's eyes and felt as if she had made a friend. So why did she also feel that somehow this woman was tricking her?

Robert sat next to Laura in the sports car. He seemed too tall for the passenger seat in this tiny car.

'How strange this is,' thought Laura. 'How odd that he is suddenly here beside me, in Nick's car, when I thought … I thought … What did I think? I thought he hated me! I thought he had no time for city people!' Then she remembered what he had said up the mountain.

'What did you mean,' she asked, 'when you said perhaps I was doing something that wasn't good for me?'

'Ah,' said Robert. 'Only you know the answer to that.'

They were silent for a few minutes as Laura drove up a small road. Then Robert said, 'OK, my house is just up this road here. Thank you very much for the lift.'

'That's OK,' Laura said as he got out.

He stood for a moment with his back to Laura, as if he was deciding what to do – to walk into his house or turn round.

Then he suddenly turned to her and said, 'I don't suppose you … you'd like a cup of tea?'

Laura looked at her watch. Nick would probably be out on the lake for another half an hour at least. She could take a few minutes to have a cup of tea with the vet. She felt pleased that he'd asked her. From what Maggie had said, he wasn't usually very sociable. Perhaps now he and Maggie were becoming close, he was learning to relax with other people. Perhaps Maggie was helping him get over Chiara at last.

Kip was barking happily and looking at Robert with an open mouth as if he was smiling.

'I think Kip's decided for me!' she said.

Robert's house was large and old, though surprisingly warm and light. He led her into a big sitting room with French windows that looked out over a beautiful view of the hills.

He disappeared through a door into what must be the kitchen, and Kip followed him, looking very much at home.

'Hey, Kip, come here,' said Laura, following the little dog, but Kip was already lying down near Robert's feet.

'He remembers,' said Robert, and he smiled. Laura hadn't seen him smile much before. He had a wide mouth, and now it lit up his face as if the sun had just come out.

'You know, I want to thank you again for saving Kip's life,' Laura said shyly, looking up at Robert.

He was pouring milk into two mugs of tea. 'It's just my job,' he said.

'Yes, but I don't know what I'd have said to Joseph if he'd died. I felt terrible. I wasn't used to having a dog. I didn't think to check the barn.' She felt nervous of Robert even now, and when she was nervous she kept talking.

'And is Joseph a very good friend?' he asked.

'Yes. He's a dear old man who lives next door to me in London. He was taken ill the night before we came here. He asked me to look after Kip for him. He said he was frightened Kip might die before he did. I think he was frightened that if Kip died, he'd have no more reason to live. He's alone. He only has his dog.'

'Let's go and sit in there,' Robert said, and they went back through to the lovely sitting room. Outside, sheets of rain moved across the hills and trees.

'So, if Kip had died, the old man would have had no reason to live,' he repeated. 'I know that feeling …'

Laura waited, realising Robert was about to tell her about Chiara, about himself. She didn't want to speak, didn't want to break the silence that waited to be filled with his words.

He was standing at the window, looking out onto the countryside. She looked at his wide shoulders in his big hand-knitted jumper; his long legs in old corduroy trousers; his fair hair that looked as if it hadn't been brushed. And suddenly she knew for certain why he made her feel so nervous. It was because she found him so attractive.

She wished she didn't. She wished she'd never seen him. She wished she'd never come on this weekend to the Lakes. Because one thing was certain. There was no way this man would ever look at her in that way. He was with Maggie now. And although things were not going well with him, she was still with Nick.

'I've been completely wrong about you,' Robert said suddenly, turning round and looking at her. 'I owe you an apology.'

'No, no, it's fine,' said Laura.

'I was rude and unpleasant to you. I thought it was you out on your jet-ski that morning. I thought it was your dog and that you didn't know how to care for him properly. I thought … I thought you just had a dog to be fashionable. But I was wrong. I hope you accept my apology,' he said.

'Of course I accept your apology,' said Laura.

'I mean … what I'm trying to say is that in fact you're the complete opposite to what I thought. You're thoughtful, and so very kind to look after this little dog for an old man on your weekend away. My problem is … my problem is I find it hard to … to … believe in anyone since my girlfriend died. I really felt I had no reason to live for a long time after she was killed.'

'That must be quite normal. Anyone would feel like that,' said Laura.

'Then my reason became stopping people jet-skiing. Apart from work, it was all I cared about,' Robert went on. 'I hated everyone that had anything to do with it. It's not good to hate people like that.'

'You couldn't help it. It's understandable. And it is awful to see jet-skis on these beautiful lakes. They look horrible and they sound terrible!' Laura said.

'I want to stop hating people all the time. I want to feel something good again. I'd like to feel …'

'What?' asked Laura quietly.

'Well, what I'm trying to say is, I think I'm beginning to feel something … for someone … again,' said Robert.

Laura suddenly felt breathless. She was afraid she was going to stop breathing altogether. She didn't want him to tell her about his feelings for Maggie. She simply didn't want to hear it. Not now she was beginning to have feelings for this man herself.

'I must go,' she said, standing up and putting her tea cup down. 'I need to get Nick from the water sports centre. Come on, Kip!'

Chapter 15 *Two goodbyes*

Laura wanted to get out of the room, out of the house, as quickly as possible. She wasn't sure where Robert was heading with his conversation, but she was afraid of it. She must go. She must go before she got in any deeper.

Robert followed her through to the front door.

'Well,' he said, 'I guess it's goodbye. Goodbye, Kip, and goodbye, Laura. When are you leaving?'

'Tomorrow,' she said. 'So goodbye. And thank you.'

He put his hand on the door. 'You're not angry? You understand what I've been trying to say?'

'Of course. We all make mistakes about people,' said Laura. 'When I first saw you in the pub, I thought you were a hill-walking poet,' she said.

He laughed. 'Well, I do enjoy hill-walking, so that part is true,' he said. 'And in fact I do write poems sometimes, so you weren't completely wrong.'

She smiled. 'I've got to go,' she said, but Robert's hand was still on the door and he hadn't opened it.

'Goodbye, Laura,' he said again, and she looked at him. And for the first time she saw that his eyes were looking right into hers.

And then she knew it was happening. She knew that there was nothing she could do to stop it. She was falling for this man. A man who was still in love with his dead girlfriend. A man who had just got together with another woman.

There were tears in her eyes as Laura drove away from Robert's house, back towards the lake.

'What has happened?' she wondered. 'How can this possibly have happened? I came here with Nick and I've fallen in love with someone else.'

She drove along angrily, and the rain fell heavily as she went.

'Normally I like someone, and then find out that I don't like them. This time I met someone who seemed to hate me, and I've found out that I like – no, I love him! Robert is so different to Nick. He's so kind! He's so thoughtful. We think like each other …'

The thoughts went round and round in her head as she drove.

'Nick isn't the person I thought he was after all, and I don't want to be with him. And Robert is someone I want to be with, but I can't! I must stop feeling anything right now.' She looked at Kip on the seat beside her. 'Help me, Kip,' she said. 'Help me to forget the vet!'

* * *

The next morning Laura and Nick got up early, ready to leave. Laura felt unhappy again. How could she sit next to Nick for another six hours in that tiny car all the way back to London? It was clear they had nothing more to say to each other. It was clear their relationship wasn't working.

'Hurry up!' said Nick. 'I don't want to get back too late. I've got a busy week.'

'OK,' said Laura. 'I'm ready. My bag's in the car. Come on, Kip!' she called. 'Time to go back to Joseph.'

Nick was just getting into the car when Laura's mobile rang. Laura answered it.

'Hello?'

'Laura Barton?' a woman asked.

'Yes,' replied Laura.

'This is Nurse Jones at St Thomas's Hospital. I believe you are a friend of Mr Joseph Donaldson?'

'Oh yes. How is he?' asked Laura.

'I'm sorry to tell you that Joseph died in the night,' the nurse said.

'What?' asked Laura quietly.

'I'm sorry. I know it's bad news, but he was very poorly and it was peaceful,' the nurse said.

Laura tried to speak, but all she could say was, 'But I have his dog.'

'Yes. Can you keep it? I'm sure Joseph would be happy for you to have it,' the nurse said.

'Oh, I'd never thought of keeping a dog. I have a small flat and …' Laura started. She could feel tears starting to run down her face.

'Anyway, I'm sorry to give you bad news,' the nurse said.

When the nurse had said goodbye, Laura sat in silence for a few moments.

'Who was that?' Nick asked.

'It was the hospital. Joseph died. They want me to keep the dog.'

'You're not keeping that dog!' said Nick. 'It's already cost you over a hundred pounds and been more trouble than it's worth.'

Laura looked at him. There were tears in her eyes.

'What's the matter?' Nick asked impatiently.

'Nick! My friend has just died. And all you can think about is how much the dog has cost me.'

'I'm sorry,' said Nick. 'I am, really. I wasn't thinking. It's just … What are you going to do with Kip in your tiny flat?'

'I don't know! I didn't expect this. I need to think for a moment.'

Laura walked up past the barn and stood looking at the view, touching Kip's head, thinking about Joseph. About the way he'd held her hand and said, 'You will take care of him, won't you?'

Kip had no idea his owner had died. It seemed so sad. 'What am I going to do with you?' she said to Kip.

Then it came to her like a bright light that made her want to jump up and run as fast as she could down the hill.

'Come on, Kip!' she said. 'We're going to see the vet again.'

Chapter 16   *At the station*

'Nick, would you mind driving me and Kip to the vet's surgery?' she asked gently.

'The vet? That vet again?' asked Nick.

'Yes, Nick, the vet again. I need to ask him if he'd like to have Kip. I've got a feeling they were meant for each other.'

'OK,' said Nick. 'You started this weekend at the vet's, so I guess it's right that you end it there too.'

'After that please could you take me to the station?' said Laura. 'I'll get the train home. I can't come back with you. You know that, don't you?'

'What are you saying, Laura? What's this about?' Nick asked.

'Look, Nick. It isn't working between us, is it? I need time to think.'

Nick looked at her. 'Is our relationship over?' he asked.

'What do you think?' Laura said.

'I should have guessed,' he said. 'This is why I don't usually bring women on holiday with me. It never works.'

'But isn't it better that we know?' said Laura. 'Isn't it better that we find out now, instead of in a year's time, that we have nothing in common?'

'I guess it is,' said Nick.

For a moment Laura felt sorry for him. It was as much of a disappointment to him as it was to her. But they both knew that she was right.

* * *

Robert looked down at Kip. 'So,' he said, 'I've got a friend at last.'

He felt near to tears. He didn't know why. He picked the dog up and it touched his cheek with its nose.

It was odd. He wasn't alone now, so why did he have a terrible feeling of emptiness, almost as bad as just after Chiara had died? It was so painful that he felt like hiding his face in Kip's fur and crying.

Then it hit him at last. It wasn't enough to have Kip. He wanted Laura too. He hated the thought that she had gone, that he would never see her again.

It was the first time he'd had feelings like this for ... how long had it been? But Laura had Nick, and they were on their way back today. Back to the city and the lives they enjoyed down there, full of money and drinking and clothes and the other things people did in the city.

*   *   *

Laura sat alone on the station platform. Nick had left her at the station and gone back to London. She felt alone.

At least she knew that Kip had found a home, the best home possible. Joseph would have been pleased, she was certain of that.

When the train came into the station at last, she got on slowly, wishing that she didn't have to leave.

She sat in a corner of the train and went over the last couple of hours in her mind. Robert had taken Kip immediately. He hardly had to be asked.

'Of course I'll have him!' he'd said, a smile lighting up his face. Laura felt again like kissing him, as she had on the first night when he'd taken Kip home with him. But Maggie had been there, watching from the door, like a silent warning.

Laura sighed.

The train hurried south between fresh green hills that rose to either side. Soon she would be back in the city, back in her shop. This weekend, the beauty of the hills, Robert and Kip would just be memories.

* * *

The morning surgery was over and Robert had gone home for lunch. The house felt so empty. Robert looked at Kip, who looked back at him questioningly.

'What have I got to lose?' he asked the little dog.

He picked up his mobile. Sure enough, Laura's mobile number was on it, on the list of people who had phoned him recently.

'Laura,' he said when she answered. 'I know this is crazy. I know I sound mad. But I just wanted to speak to you again.' There were a few seconds of silence.

'Are you home yet?' he asked.

'No, I didn't drive back with Nick. I'm on a train. Nick and I are finished. I didn't want to go back with him.'

'A train? What …? What's the next station?' Robert asked.

'Oxenholme,' Laura replied.

'Oxenholme? Can you get off there? Get off and wait for me! I'll come and get you. We need to talk,' Robert said quickly. 'You know something's happening between us, don't you?'

'Robert, I can't. I've got to get back to London. Jo is expecting me back in the shop tomorrow.'

'You can get a later train. Please,' said Robert.

Laura listened to his voice. How could she fight it?

'OK,' she said at last. 'I'll get off at Oxenholme.'

'Wait at the station,' said Robert. 'I'll be there as soon as I can.'

* * *

Laura sat on the station platform at Oxenholme feeling cold. 'What am I doing?' she wondered. 'Am I crazy? I need to be at work tomorrow. But I need to see Robert again. And he wants to see me! I can't possibly let him go.'

At last she looked up to see Robert and Kip coming towards her, and she knew after all she was doing the right thing.

Robert ran up to her on the platform and put his arms around her.

'The minute you left, I knew I couldn't just let you go,' he said. 'Will you come back with me, just for a few hours? You can get a later train.'

'But … but what will Maggie say?' she asked.

'Maggie? My receptionist? What do you mean, what will she say?' Robert asked.

'I thought you and she were … I thought … Aren't you going out with her?'

Robert put his head back and laughed.

'I'm sorry,' he said. 'I can't think of a crazier idea! It's you I like. It's you I need. I haven't felt like this for years.'

Before she could argue Laura found herself next to Robert in the Land Rover, driving away from the station.

As Robert drove down the small road towards the lake, he tried not to think of that night two years ago. He put his hand on Kip's head as they came through the trees towards the lake. He held his breath as he waited for it to happen. The thing that always happened. The terrible sounds, the lights and screams.

They were beside the lake now. He waited. There was nothing.

He looked out across the water. Nothing. Just the light of the afternoon sun shining gently on the still water.

It was silent. It was beautiful. He felt odd, as if he was lighter than he'd been before. He felt as if his chest was full.

'What is this?' he thought. 'What's happening?'

And then he realised. He felt happy. For the first time in two years he felt happy.

He reached out his hand again and took Laura's hand, and then he looked at her and she smiled.

'You know when you offered to take Kip home with you after he ate the poison?' Laura said. 'I wanted to kiss you.'

'Why didn't you?' asked Robert.

'Because I thought you hated me,' she said.

He stopped the Land Rover then and moved towards her. 'You can kiss me now,' he said.

And the sun lit up their faces as they kissed.